Overcoming the Odds

Lee Trevino

Jon Kramer

RSVP

RAINTREE
STECK-VAUGHN
PUBLISHERS
The Steck-Vaughn Company

Austin, Texas

Published by Raintree Steck-Vaughn Publishers,
an imprint of Steck-Vaughn Company

Developed for Steck-Vaughn Company by
Visual Education Corporation, Princeton, New Jersey
Project Director: Paula McGuire
Editor: Marilyn Miller
Photo Research: Marty Levick
Electronic Preparation: Cynthia C. Feldner
Production Supervisor: Barbara A. Kopel
Electronic Production: Lisa Evans-Skopas, Christine Osborne
Interior Design: Maxson Crandall

Raintree Steck-Vaughn Publishers staff
Editor: Helene Resky
Project Manager: Joyce Spicer

Photo Credits: **Cover:** © David Cannon/ALLSPORT USA;
4: © Walter Iooss, Jr./*Sports Illustrated/TIME INC.;* **6:** © UPI/Bettmann;
13: © AP/Wide World Photos, Inc.; **17:** © James Drake/*Sports Illustrated/TIME INC.;*
19: © Walter Iooss, Jr./*Sports Illustrated/TIME INC.;* **20:** © UPI/Bettmann;
21: © Gerry Cranham/*Sports Illustrated/TIME INC.;* **22:** © George Long/*Sports Illustrated/TIME INC.;*
24: © Gerry Cranham/*Sports Illustrated/Time Inc.;*
25: © Marvin E. Newman/*Sports Illustrated/TIME INC.;* **30:** © David Cannon/ALLSPORT USA;
31: © Wide World Photos, Inc.; **33:** © David Cannon/ALLSPORT USA;
35: © Stephen Wade/ALLSPORT USA; **37:** © Gary Newkirk/ALLSPORT USA;
41: © Wide World Photos, Inc.; **42:** © AP/Wide World Photos, Inc.; **43:** © ALLSPORT USA

Library of Congress Cataloging-in-Publication Data
Kramer, Jon.
 Lee Trevino/ Jon Kramer.
  p.   cm. — (Overcoming the odds)
 Includes bibliographical references (p.   ) and index.
 Summary: A biography of the Mexican-American professional golfer who made a
comeback after being struck by lightning.
 ISBN 0-8172-4124-8 (hardcover)
 1. Trevino, Lee—Juvenile literature.   2. Golfers—United States—Biography—
Juvenile literature.   [1. Trevino, Lee.   2. Golfers.   3. Mexican Americans—
Biography.]   I. Title.   II. Series.
GV964.T73K73 1996
796.352′092—dc20
[B]
                                                                      95–45388
                                                                         CIP
                                                                          AC

Printed and bound in the United States
1 2 3 4 5 6 7 8 9 0   WZ   99 98 97 96 95

Table of contents

Chapter 1

"The Merry Mex"

Few people have played golf better than Lee Trevino. In 22 years of play he has won an astonishing 27 tournaments on the Professional Golfer's Association (PGA) Tour. Few people have also ever had more fun on a golf course than Lee Trevino. Indeed, the media have called the Mexican-American Trevino "The Merry Mex." But in June 1975, the laughter stopped, and Lee Trevino had to face the greatest obstacle in his life.

Lee was playing in the Western Open in suburban Chicago. He was on the 13th green with fellow golfers Jerry Heard and Bobby Nichols when disaster struck.

It was raining hard at the time. Play was stopped as the golfers waited out the storm. They should have taken shelter. It can be dangerous to be out during a storm.

Lee was leaning on his golf bag by the edge of the green. Heard and Nichols were not far from him. Suddenly, lightning skipped off a nearby lake.

Lee is having fun all dressed up in Mexican clothing at the 1968 Tournament of Champions.

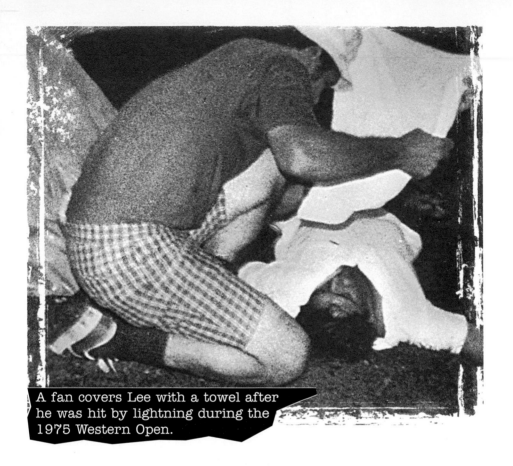

A fan covers Lee with a towel after he was hit by lightning during the 1975 Western Open.

It traveled through the ground and up the metal shafts of Lee's golf clubs. A moment later, Lee was in the air. The bolt struck his back and sent him flying. Lee was knocked to the ground.

"The pain in my left arm and shoulder was killing me, but I kept fighting it," said Lee. He was lying on his back with his left arm twisted underneath him. Soon help arrived. Lee was rushed to the hospital. He had four burn marks on his shoulder where the lightning left his body.

Lee was examined at the hospital. He had numbness on his left side and was having trouble breathing. "I can't tell you a lot about lightning," said the doctor. She told Lee, "You're one of the few to get hit and survive it."

Lee spent several days in the hospital. The shock had damaged some muscles in his body. "My accident had been like a child cutting himself," said Lee. "At that particular moment it doesn't scare you. It's always afterward, when you realize what could have happened, that you feel afraid."

Lee made a quick recovery and resumed his career. A few weeks later, he headed to the British Open in Scotland.

"I didn't play well," Lee said, "but I was just delighted to be there, alive and laughing."

His ability to laugh and his determination have always helped Lee overcome many other obstacles. He developed severe back problems in the months following the accident. He had to undergo surgery several times to repair the damage. Each time he had surgery, he came back and played better than ever.

Lee had more physical problems after joining the Senior Tour in 1989. A golfer becomes eligible to play the Senior Tour when he turns 50. Lee missed some time in 1993 after undergoing thumb surgery. That could have ended his career. Like an artist, a golfer needs full use of his hands. But Lee bounced back yet again. He won nearly a million dollars in 1993.

Lee faced another test at the end of 1994. This time, he needed delicate surgery on his neck.

The first tournament of 1995 was held in Puerto Rico. Lee returned to the game with a steel plate in his neck. He was still getting his strength back. But Lee put on a great show and almost won the event!

Off the course, Lee has also had to overcome obstacles. His first two marriages ended in divorce. He also lost some money in bad investments. Despite that, Lee remains one of the happiest people around. He is also one of the greatest golfers of his time.

"Golf is all I know, all I want to do," he says. "I can't wait to wake up in the morning because I know I'm going to play golf. I love to play. I want to play every day and hopefully I'll be able to play for many years to come."

Lee has won over $8 million since joining the PGA Tour in 1967. He owns a home in Jupiter Island, a wealthy resort in Florida. He is also one of golf's most popular players. Golf has given him the chance to make friends all over the world. But before he could even start to play golf, Lee needed to overcome his first obstacle—growing up in poverty.

Chapter 2

Lee's Humble Beginnings

Lee Trevino was born on December 1, 1939, in Dallas, Texas. He was raised by his mother, Juanita, and his grandfather, Joe. Lee never knew his father. His parents never married, so he was given his mother's name of Trevino.

Lee and his sisters Anna and Josephine lived in a four-room house without electricity or indoor plumbing. It was located in a hay field near the Glen Lakes Country Club.

Lee's mother cleaned houses in North Dallas. His grandfather worked as a gravedigger. Joe never made more than $40 a week. Neither he nor Lee's mother could read or write. Lee's grandfather worked very hard to support the family. "My grandfather was the best father I could have ever had," said Lee. "He was unbelievable."

Life was tough for the Trevino family. "My Uncle Lupe lived with us and he had his own room," said Lee. "The rest of us slept in one room, my grandfather using our only real mattress. On cold nights my mother and us kids would sleep together in one bed on old canvas sacks stuffed with dry grass. We put a huge log in the stove that would burn half the night. Then someone got up in the freezing cold to start another fire."

The family used lake water to wash clothes and take baths. Lee's grandfather took drinking water home from the cemetery in five-gallon drums. The Trevinos also used the drinking water for all their cooking. There were no cabinets. Their closet was nothing more than a few nails on the wall.

Lee started hanging out at Glen Lakes when he was eight years old. He began by caddying for some of the members. A caddie is someone who carries a golfer's bag. He walks side by side with the player for the entire round. A caddie cleans the golfer's clubs and provides advice when needed. The golfer usually gives him a tip when the round is finished. Lee used his tips to help out his family.

"I caddied primarily for the same men all the time," said Lee. "They seemed to like me. I was a good caddie, a hustling kid who didn't mind the work. If they wanted to hit balls late, I went out and chased them until dark."

Soon Lee was playing golf against other caddies. They had a little three-hole layout behind the shed where they hung out. Sometimes, a member would let Lee hit a few shots on the regular course when no one was looking. He soon fell in love with the game. He learned to play well and practice hard.

Lee skipped school quite a bit. He finally dropped out before entering the eighth grade. "Today, I feel much differently about education," he says. "I will not tolerate my children missing school and not getting an excellent education. But then, my mind was somewhere else."

At the age of 14, Lee got his first full-time job. He caddied and worked as a member of the greens crew at Glen Lakes Country Club. The greens crew cuts the grass and takes care of the golf course. When Lee had time, he hung out at Hardy's Driving Range. The owner, Hardy Greenwood, had a big impact on Lee's life.

Lee had caught Hardy's attention several years earlier when Lee began hitting balls at the age of eight. Hardy thought Lee was a natural. He told him he had a real future in the game.

Hardy gave Lee a job at the range. The young Trevino picked up balls for a dollar an hour. He worked six days a week and practiced when he could. When Lee was 15, Hardy signed him up for a junior tournament. He gave Lee a full set of clubs and a pair of spiked golf shoes.

Lee had hit millions of balls by then. But he had never played a complete round of golf. He qualified for the tournament by shooting 77. That means Lee had taken 77 strokes to complete all 18 holes. It was a great score for someone so young. Touring pros usually shoot in the low 70s.

Lee grew restless as a teenager. In 1956, at the age of 17, he left Hardy's and joined the United States Marine Corps for a little more than three years. After going through training camp in California, Lee was stationed in Japan. While there, he played on the Marine golf team. It was during this time that he became really serious about the game.

Lee served in the Marines until 1960. After his discharge, he returned to Hardy's Driving Range back home. He helped build a pitch-and-putt golf course with Hardy Greenwood. A pitch-and-putt is a shorter version of a regular course. Hardy asked Lee to come back and work for him full time. "You have the ability to become a professional golfer and a good one," he told Lee. "You can work nights and have your days free to play golf."

Lee turned pro a short time later, in 1960. He spent a lot of time at Tenison Park, a public course in Dallas. "A lot of wealthy people played there," said Lee, "some for fun, some for big money. Tenison was the only golf course I've ever seen where the parking lot was filled with Cadillacs, jalopies, pickups, and beverage trucks."

Lee liked to hustle in those early days. He'd play anyone for money. Lee especially needed money because he now had a family to support. In 1962, he married his first wife, Linda. They had a son named Richard that same year before divorcing. Less than a year later, Lee married his second wife, Claudia. She

In 1970 Lee sat for this family photo with his wife Claudia, who is holding their son Tony. The other children are Richard, on the right, and Leslie, who is next to Claudia's mother, on Lee's lap.

went by the nickname of "Clyde." Lee and Claudia had three children—Leslie Ann, Tony Lee, and Troy.

In the early sixties, it wasn't easy to join the professional tour. Golfers were supposed to have five years of club pro experience. But Lee felt he was ready to play against the best in the world. Hardy disagreed. He refused to sign the papers that said Lee had the necessary experience. Hardy thought Lee was too young to go on the road. He felt Lee was too immature to handle the responsibility.

In February 1966, Lee, Claudia, and their baby daughter Leslie moved to El Paso, a city in west Texas about 650 miles (1,045 km) from Dallas. It's just over the border from Mexico. Lee found a job at Horizon Hills Country Club, where he continued to play anyone for money.

One time, a young pro named Raymond Floyd came to visit. Floyd eventually became one of the greatest golfers of his time. But, in those days, Floyd liked to travel in search of a match. He was a cocky player who didn't think anyone could beat him. When Floyd visited El Paso, the members at Horizon Hills arranged a little match. Floyd drove up to the club and was met by a young man in a golf cart. The man carried Floyd's clubs into the locker room and cleaned his shoes.

"So who am I going to be playing against?" Floyd asked the man. "Me," said Lee. Floyd was stunned. He could not believe that the clubhouse attendant was his competition. What a joke, he thought.

The joke was on Floyd. He and Lee played for three days in a row. The objective in golf is to complete a round in the fewest number of strokes. On the first day Floyd shot 67, but Lee beat him with a 65. Floyd was mad. He wanted to play some more that day.

Lee said "no." He told Floyd, "I can't play another nine. I've got to put the carts up, clean the clubs, and all that other stuff." Floyd shook his head. He said, "I can't believe this. Here I am playing a cart man, a bag-storage man, and I can't beat him."

On the second day Floyd shot 66, but Lee responded with another 65. On the final day, Floyd broke through. He beat Lee by a shot to save some dignity. "I can find easier games than this," said the touring pro. "I have had enough."

Chapter 3

Becoming a Pro

Lee knew he was ready for the big time. He finally got his Class A card in May 1967. This card enabled him to play the PGA Tour. The PGA Tour is a series of competitions that the best golfers play during the year. Lee's application was endorsed by Bill Eschenbrenner, the head pro at El Paso Country Club.

That year, Lee qualified for the U.S. Open. The U.S. Open is a major tournament, perhaps the most important on the PGA schedule. The 1967 Open was held at Baltusrol Golf Club in Springfield, New Jersey. Lee's friends came up with the money for his plane ticket. It was his first trip east of the Mississippi River.

Lee arrived with six shirts, three pairs of slacks, his clubs, and one pair of golf shoes. He may not have had much in the way of clothes, but he quickly showed he had a lot of talent. Most golf tournaments consist of four rounds that are played from Thursday to Sunday. Lee surprised everyone by shooting rounds of 72-70-71-70 for a total of 283. Lee finished fifth—eight strokes behind winner Jack Nicklaus.

Suddenly, Lee found himself with $6,000. This was more money than he had ever seen in his life. "I'll always remember those days at Baltusrol," said Lee. "It was one of those times when my life took a new direction."

Lee remained on the tour for the rest of 1967. He earned $26,472 that year to finish 45th on the PGA money list. Lee and Claudia traveled from tournament to tournament in a 1965 Plymouth station wagon. Most of the other golfers flew on planes. Jack Nicklaus and Arnold Palmer really traveled in style. They owned their own aircraft.

Lee was proving himself against the best in the world. Now he was ready to win. The 1968 U.S. Open was held at Oak Hill Country Club in Rochester, New York. Lee arrived in a bad mood. He had finished second in two tournaments leading up to the U.S. Open. Most golfers would have been happy with that but not Lee. He cared only about winning.

Lee got off to a good start in Rochester, shooting rounds of 68 and 69. He trailed leader Bert Yancey by two strokes midway through the event. On Saturday, Lee shot 69 to cut Yancey's lead to one shot.

Lee and Yancey were paired for the final round. Both were feeling the pressure. Lee took the lead when Yancey bogeyed the fifth hole.

In golf, par is the number of strokes an expert golfer is expected to take on a given hole. Each hole is given a par of three, four, or five, depending on its length or difficulty. If, for instance, a golfer takes a five on a par-4, it's called a bogey (one over par). If a golfer completes a par-4 in two shots, he or she has earned an eagle (two under par). If a golfer completes a par-4 in three shots, it's called a birdie (one under par).

Every golfer tries to take the fewest strokes possible. Eagles are great, birdies are very good, pars are good, and bogeys are bad.

Lee played extremely well that Sunday afternoon. He went to the final hole with a four-shot lead. "I don't remember very much. I guess I was in shock. I know I wasn't saying much," said the usually talkative Trevino.

Lee is playing in the 1968 U.S. Open Golf Championship. This was Lee's first win on the Professional Golfer's Association (PGA) Tour.

With his final-round 69, Lee won the tournament. He also became the first player in U.S. Open history to play all four rounds with scores in the 60s. His victory was worth $30,000 in prize money. Lee had finally crashed the winner's circle, and in the U.S. Open, too!

It's rare for a player to earn his first tour win in that event. The courses are tough, and the pressure is intense. The winner is usually someone with lots of experience.

"I never dreamed that tournament would do so much for my career," said Lee. "It gave me a tremendous amount of confidence, because it was the first event I ever won and because of the caliber of the golf course, tournament, and players. And since it was the U.S. Open, it gave me the impression that other tournaments wouldn't be as hard to win."

From 1968 through 1971, Lee won ten major tour events. He also finished second eight times and third on eleven occasions. Lee was named to a pair of Ryder Cup teams and competed in four World Cup tournaments. The Ryder Cup matches a team of U.S. golfers against a team from Europe. It's a high-pressure event that's held every two years. The World Cup is a two-man competition featuring golfers from several different countries.

Lee won the Vardon Trophy in 1970 and 1971. This trophy is given to the player with the lowest scoring average on tour.

Lee was also winning a lot of money. He won $132,127 in 1968. The next year he earned $112,418. In 1970, he was the tour's leading money winner, bringing home $157,037.

When Lee arrived at the 1971 U.S. Open, he was playing as well as anyone. He had won the Tallahassee Open in April and the Memphis Classic in May. Lee had finished second twice and third in three other events.

The 1971 U.S. Open was held at Merion Golf Club, just outside Philadelphia, Pennsylvania. It was a short course. Merion had narrow fairways with high rough. Golfers like to keep the ball in the fairway, or short grass, and out of the rough, or long, thick grass. It is much easier to control the ball from the fairway. The Merion course was perfectly suited to Lee's game. Lee wasn't the longest hitter, but he was deadly accurate.

Lee is on his way to winning the 1971 U.S. Open.

After three rounds, Lee was four shots behind leader Jim Simons. He was two behind his great rival Jack Nicklaus. Simons faltered on Sunday, while Lee shot a 70 and Nicklaus a 72. Lee and Nicklaus were tied after four rounds. They were to have an 18-hole play-off the following day.

"My chances are just as good as Jack's," said Lee. "The pressure is on him. He's the best ever, the odds-on favorite. If I lose, people expect it. If he loses, it makes me look like a hero."

Five minutes before the start of the play-off, Lee decided to relieve the tension. He reached into his golf bag and pulled out a rubber snake. Lee waved it at Nicklaus. The two cracked up laughing.

Lee has just picked up the toy snake to relieve tension during the 1971 U.S. Open.

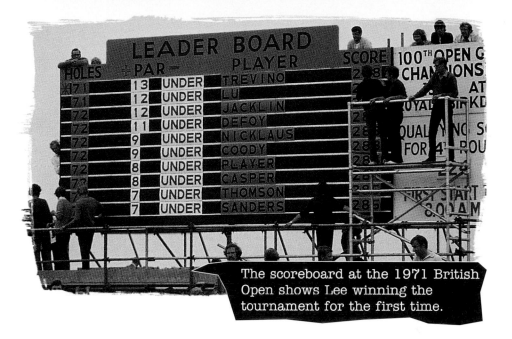

LEADER BOARD

HOLES +PAR- PLAYER SCORE 100TH OPEN G

471 13 UNDER TREVINO 28 CHAMPIONS
71 12 UNDER LU AT
72 12 UNDER JACKLIN ROYAL BIR KD
72 11 UNDER DEFOY 28 QUALI YING S
72 9 UNDER NICKLAUS 28 FOR 4 ROU
72 9 UNDER COODY 28
72 8 UNDER PLAYER 28
72 8 UNDER CASPER FIRST START
73 7 UNDER THOMSON 8:00 AM
7 UNDER SANDERS 285

The scoreboard at the 1971 British Open shows Lee winning the tournament for the first time.

Lee took an early lead in the play-off and coasted to victory. "Winning this Open means a great deal more to me than winning in 1968 at Oak Hill," he said. "I think it was the champion golfer Walter Hagen who said, 'Any man can win one Open, but it takes a great player to win two.'"

In his next start, Lee won the Canadian Open. He did it in another play-off, this time with Art Wall. Only six days later, he birdied the final hole to win the British Open at Royal Birkdale, England. Lee was on quite a roll. Up to that point, only four men—Tommy Armour, Bobby Jones, Ben Hogan, and Gene Sarazen—had ever won two national titles in the same year. Lee became the first to win three.

"It's fantastic," said Lee, after defeating a star-studded field in England. "The odds were all against me after winning the U.S. Open and the Canadian Open. But I like bucking the odds, and this is the title I've always wanted to win. I've never won across the water before."

Lee realized his life was changing. "I used to tell jokes, and nobody laughed," he said. "Now I tell the same jokes, and they crack up. I had no car; now I have five. I used to live in a two-bed trailer; now I am building a five-bedroom house. I didn't have a phone. Now I have an unlisted number. Boy, that's progress." The little boy who had slept on old canvas sacks had come a long way.

In 1971, the city of El Paso celebrates Lee's great year with a Lee Trevino Day. Lee is in the car, waving to bystanders.

Chapter 4

A Bolt of Lightning

Lee was at the peak of his career in 1972. He defended his British Open title at Muirfield, Scotland. Showing plenty of guts in the final round, Lee chipped in to save par on the 17th hole. Another par on the final hole made him the winner. Lee became the first player since Arnold Palmer in 1962 to successfully defend the British Open championship.

For someone who grew up in Texas, Lee adapted well to British golf. "I love this championship," he said. "I love the links courses, with the mist and the wind sweeping off the sea."

"There's nothing quite like playing in the British Isles," he added. "Golf is in the air there. You breathe it, like the smell of home cooking. It makes you hungry. You want to play."

Lee won his third straight Vardon Trophy in 1972. At the 1973 Memphis Classic, he reached another milestone. With his second-place finish, Lee reached the $1 million mark in official earnings. It took him 6 years and 11 months to achieve this goal. No one had ever done it quicker.

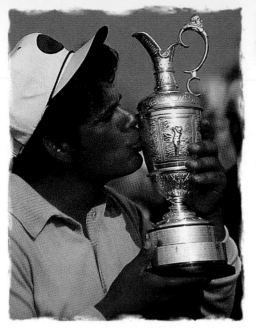

Lee won yet another duel with Jack Nicklaus in North Carolina at the 1974 PGA Championship. It marked the fourth year in a row that he brought home more than $200,000 in official earnings.

During the week of the PGA Championship, Lee rented a house from a woman named Mrs. Mayberry. He was having putting problems at the time and was looking for a cure.

While strolling through the house, Lee found an old putter that had belonged to Mrs. Mayberry's husband. Lee liked the feel of it. He asked Mrs. Mayberry if he could buy the putter. She smiled and said, "If you win the tournament, I'll give it to you."

The old putter worked wonders. Lee won his fifth major title.

Lee was a popular champion. He loved to crack jokes and banter with the fans. But Lee was deadly serious when he had to be. One PGA official said that Lee was the only guy out there who has all the shots and will play them under pressure. And Nicklaus once said, "There are a lot of fine strikers of the ball.

Trevino is a fine striker and a fine thinker. He knows what he's doing all the time."

Golf can be a very serious sport. Most players need complete silence to concentrate. Lee played better when he was relaxed. Some golfers found it difficult to play with him because he was always yakking between shots. However, the fans loved him. In golf, a group of fans that follows a particular player is called a "gallery." Arnold Palmer was supported by "Arnie's Army." Trevino's group was called "Lee's Fleas."

Lee's fans are called "Lee's Fleas." Here they watch their hero have a little fun on the golf course.

Lee needed all the support he could get to make it through the darkest period of his life. It began in June 1975 when he was struck by that bolt of lightning at the Western Open outside Chicago.

After being hit, Lee spent 24 hours in the intensive care unit of an Illinois hospital. Doctors were fearful that the shock had damaged his heart. Luckily, that was not the case. Lee returned to action three weeks later. But things weren't right. He complained of weakness.

Lee won a tournament in 1976. But several months later, he experienced terrible back pain. The pain returned again and again. It got so bad that Lee couldn't swing a club. That November, he underwent an operation to relieve the pain.

Lee believed that the shock caused by the lightning damaged the disks that protect the back's vertebrae. He also thought it weakened the muscles surrounding his spine.

All golfers experience back pain at one time or another. The twists and turns of the swing can cause problems if you're not in shape. Lee's back trouble never really went away. "You wouldn't believe the pain I feel every morning when I wake up, even now," he said in 1977.

Lee was able to overcome his pain. He followed a program of physical exercise. The hard work paid off. Lee captured his second Canadian Open title in July 1977. "When you've been hurt bad, you want to prove you can win again," he said after an emotional final round. "And there were times when it came into my mind that I might not do it."

Getting struck by lightning is one of the scarier things a person can experience. Lee realized that it was a turning point in his life. "I got it all too fast. Stardom, recognition, whatever," he said. "It went to my head."

"I was neglecting practice, making excuses, turning into a give-up artist," he continued. "When I got hit by lightning in 1975 and then had the back surgery in 1976, it gave me almost a whole year to take a good look at myself. I realized that for years I'd been floating away from hard work. I was getting away from the one thing I believed in."

Lee had another distraction. In the late 1970s, he was experiencing some financial problems. Lee figures he lost $1.5 million because of poor business deals. He had to sell off most of what he owned or had invested in.

A lesser man would have been angry. Lee decided to work that much harder. He played some of his best golf in the period from 1978 to 1980. Competing near his hometown of Dallas, Lee won the 1978 Colonial National Invitational in Fort Worth. By the time 1978 had ended, he had added five second-place finishes to his record.

In 1979, Lee won his third Canadian Open title. With this win, he became just the second man to earn more than $2 million on the PGA Tour. Jack Nicklaus was the first. It was Lee's 22nd tour victory. But he was itching for more. "Now I'm going for $3 million," he said. "There's always a goal, always something else to try for."

Lee had a brilliant season in 1980. Now 40 years old, he won three events—the Tournament Players Championship, the San Antonio–Texas Open, and the Memphis Classic. Lee earned $385,814 in prize money. His stroke average of 69.73 was the best on the tour. In the same year he also won the Ben Hogan Award, given to a golfer who overcomes a serious injury. Hogan was a magnificent player who was nearly killed in a 1949 auto accident. He went on to win the U.S. Open a year later.

Lee completed a terrific run by winning the 1981 Tournament of Champions. He had to defeat his old friend Raymond Floyd down the stretch. Two weeks later, though, Lee's back started to act up.

"There were times I couldn't even put my socks on," he said. "The pain was killing me. It was so bad, I really thought about giving up golf."

Lee visited several doctors. He finally found one that discovered the problem. A nerve in Lee's back had swollen to three times its normal size. He underwent another operation. The doctor promised that Lee would be able to resume his career afterward. Lee's future lay in the balance.

Chapter 5

An Unexpected Victory

Lee suffered through a painful 1981. But his spirits soared when he was named to the PGA Hall of Fame and the World Golf Hall of Fame. Receiving that honor meant that he'd be remembered as one of the greatest players in the history of the game.

Unlike other athletes who play professional baseball, football, or hockey, golfers can compete at any age. No one has to retire. If you're good, you can play as long as you want. After his second back operation, Lee struggled to regain his touch. In 1982, he entered 20 tournaments. But Lee finished in the top ten only once. His winning days seemed to be over.

For that reason, Lee began a "new" career in the broadcast booth. He did not officially retire from the PGA Tour. But he took a job with NBC sports. Lee was assigned to describe the 18th-hole play. His love of talk made him a natural for television. Lee once said, "I can't wait to get up in the morning so I can hear what I'm going to say."

"I took the job with NBC because I didn't know if I could win anymore," said Lee. He felt that he had to look for another way to make money.

Lee's job paid him good money. But he missed the competition of the tour. Lee especially missed the head-to-head duels with Raymond Floyd and Jack Nicklaus. For competitors like Lee, there's only one place, and that's first place. Those days seemed long gone. But the 44-year-old wanted one more shot at the top. Lee set his sights on the 1984 PGA Championship to be held in Birmingham, Alabama.

The Birmingham Shoal Creek Country Club was a real challenge. Jack Nicklaus designed the course.

It is long and tough. Lee was able to conquer it by shooting 69 in the first round, 68 in the second, and a record-setting 67 in the third. He began Sunday's final round in first place. Lee had a one-stroke lead over Lanny Wadkins and a two-stroke margin over Gary Player.

The 1984 PGA Championship was Lee's last big win on the PGA Tour. The win made him feel confident again.

Lee was in top form. He shot 69 on that final day to win by four strokes. When Lee sunk his final putt on the 18th hole, he kissed his putter four times. He said he did this because he was too old to jump up and down.

Lee finished at 15 under par. He became the first golfer in the history of the PGA Championship to shoot four rounds with scores in the 60s. Sixteen years earlier, he had achieved the same distinction in the U.S. Open.

"The PGA absolutely gave me new life," said Lee. "I never really got depressed about my game, but I was sure worried. It had been so long since I had won."

Lee gave much of the credit to his new wife, Claudia. She had the same first name as Lee's second wife, whom he had divorced in 1982. Claudia

Lee puts his arm around his wife Claudia. Before the 1984 PGA Championship, she gave him a pep talk that helped him go on to win.

had been a fan of Lee's. They became friends first, and then after a while they began dating. Their marriage took place in 1983. Before the 1984 PGA, Claudia gave Lee a pep talk that helped his game. "I mentioned that maybe my age was a problem out there," Lee said. Claudia replied, "Those clubs don't know how old you are."

The 1984 PGA Championship was Lee's last big victory on the PGA Tour. He won 27 tour events and finished in the top ten an amazing 167 times. From 1968 to 1981, Lee cashed at least one winner's check for 14 consecutive years. He won six "major" titles—two U.S. Opens, two British Opens, and two PGAs. Lee also played in five World Cups and six Ryder Cups, and won the Vardon Trophy for the lowest scoring average five times.

Golf's "grand slam" consists of four major tournaments—the three that Lee won and the one that he didn't, the Masters. The Masters is held every April at the Augusta National Golf Club in Augusta, Georgia. Lee never did well there. He wasn't comfortable with the course, which favored longer hitters.

His big PGA wins behind him, Lee entered a new stage in his career. When Lee was in his late forties, he turned his attention to the Senior PGA Tour, a schedule of tournaments for players 50 years or older. The courses are shorter. But the prize money is excellent. The Senior Tour has grown rapidly since

Lee is playing in the 1989 Masters Tournament. He is trying to figure how to get out of a sand trap. In a golf course, a sand trap is a shallow pit that is partly filled with sand. It is designed to serve as a hazard for the golfer.

its formation in 1980. Most players can't wait until they become eligible.

Lee was no exception. He said, "Why do I want to play with the flat bellies [on the regular tour] when I can play with the round ones?"

Chapter 6

Life After 50

Lee became eligible for the Senior Tour on December 1, 1989, when he turned 50. His first victory came in the opening event of 1990. It was the Royal Caribbean Classic in Key Biscayne, Florida. Then he won again two weeks later. In 9 of his first 11 rounds on the Senior Tour, Lee shot in the 60s.

"Trevino is in a league by himself," said golfer Chi Chi Rodriguez. "We don't even count him. We figure when you come in second, you're a winner."

As the weather got warmer, Lee got better and better. He played 26 events in 1990 and won 7 of them. Winning two or three events on the Senior Tour is considered very good. Winning seven is extraordinary. One win was in the U.S. Senior Open. That tournament was held at the Ridgewood Country Club in Paramus, New Jersey.

Once again, Lee found himself in a battle with Jack Nicklaus. Lee trailed Nicklaus by one shot as the final round began. He took an early lead and held on as Nicklaus bogeyed the second-to-last hole. "Never in my wildest dreams did I expect Jack

Lee is playing in the 1990 Seniors Tour. In his first year, he won over $1 million.

to bogey the 17th hole," said Lee. "It's great to beat him again. It's always a feather in your cap to beat Jack Nicklaus because he's the best. I was on a mission today."

In 1990, Lee won a total of $1,190,518. It had taken him nearly seven years to win his first million on the regular tour. Now competing for a lot more money, he shattered that mark as a senior. In fact, Lee won more money than any other golfer in 1990. He took in even more than Greg Norman, the leader on the regular tour.

When Lee's back started acting up at the start of 1991, his fellow golfers told a joke. They said Lee must have hurt himself trying to carry home all his trophies. He collected a few more in 1991. Lee won three events that year, totaling $723,163 in prize money. He moved into fifth place on the Senior Tour money list.

Golfers like Lee are never satisfied. They always think they can do a little better. As he began the 1992 season, Lee was determined to regain the form he displayed in 1990.

Lee blew away the competition in 1992. He won five tour events, including three in a row—The Tradition, the PGA Seniors Championship, and the Las Vegas Senior Classic. His earnings climbed to $1,027,002. Lee had become the first golfer to crack the million-dollar mark in two different seasons. He also won his third straight Byron Nelson Trophy, given to the player with the lowest scoring average on the Senior Tour.

Lee accomplished all that despite being bothered by his left thumb, which he had injured playing golf. The injury made it difficult for him to grip the club.

Lee underwent surgery to fix the problem. In golf, "feel" is everything. A player needs full use of

his or her hands. But obstacles simply made Lee more determined. Just as he had done so many times in the past, Lee came back better than ever.

It took a little bit of time, though. Lee didn't make his first 1993 start until the end of March. He won the Cadillac NFL Classic in May. But then he struggled before improving his game at the end of the season. Lee posted six top-ten finishes in his final six events. Included in that stretch were wins at the Nationwide and Vantage championships.

Lee was on quite a roll. He kept it up in 1994. He won the Royal Caribbean Classic in February. He followed that win with five more titles, including another PGA Seniors Championship. Once again, Lee earned more than $1 million. In the 1994 season, he

37

won a career-high $1,202,369 in official earnings. It was no surprise that he was named Senior Tour Player of the Year for the third time.

Lee was also enjoying life away from the course. He and Claudia liked spending time with their two children, Olivia and Lee Daniel.

Things were going as well as possible. Then, Lee had another setback. This time, the problem was neck pain that bothered him more as he grew older. He underwent delicate surgery at the end of 1994. Doctors inserted a steel plate in his neck to help speed the healing.

Lee's fellow golfers know he has the heart of a lion. Just months after the surgery, he returned to the Senior Tour. Lee's first tournament was in Puerto Rico. He had trouble keeping up with the longer hitters. Lee couldn't drive the ball as far as he wanted to. He had to rely on his intelligence and his touch around the greens.

It was amazing that so soon after surgery, Lee played well enough to have had a chance to win the tournament. Unfortunately, he fell short. But his gutsy performance served as a warning to his fellow competitors. Don't ever count Lee Trevino out! The man who dominated the Senior Tour during the 1990s is far from finished.

Chapter 7

How Lee Changed the Game of Golf

Golf has grown rapidly over the past 30 years. New courses have been built, and more and more people are playing the game. Lee Trevino helped spark this incredible surge in popularity. He won major tournaments and proved that anyone can succeed with hard work.

In the 1970s, golfer Frank Beard said, "Lee practices more than any human being I know. The man works." Lee knows that youngsters, especially Mexican Americans, look up to him. A friend of his once said, "Every time Lee talks about winning, it is of the hard work it took to get ahead. He is talking to those kids who are living the way he used to, telling them what they must do."

Lee grew up without a father. As a little boy, golf gave him an opportunity to make friends as well as money. It also gave him the excitement of competition. It's something he still feels today.

Most people would tell you that Jack Nicklaus is the greatest golfer of all time. He won 18 major titles and dominated the sport like no one else. Nicklaus and Lee had some classic battles over the years. They are still competing today on the Senior Tour.

Jack Nicklaus and Lee Trevino come from two completely different backgrounds. Nicklaus grew up in Columbus, Ohio. His father owned a chain of successful pharmacies. The younger Nicklaus learned the game at a private club and had a well-known teacher. He had a great amateur career and won his first U.S. Open at the age of 21.

Lee joined the tour at the age of 27. He won his first event a year later. Lee was basically self-taught. He has a unique, flat swing that won't work for anyone else. It's not something you'll see in a textbook.

The Trevino-Nicklaus rivalry has always been friendly. They seem to bring out the best in one another. Nicklaus has won more money and more tournaments. Lee, however, has always done well in their head-to-head matches.

"Each of us respects the other's game," Lee once said in an interview. "I consider myself a very capable shotmaker, but I would never put myself in the same class with Jack Nicklaus as a golfer.

"There are several reasons, I think, why I've done so well when we've met," Lee added. "First, he'd already scaled the heights. He had everything to lose and nothing to gain. I started with a big advantage. I was the underdog. I've always had the underdog image. I enjoy that role."

Lee is shown with one of his friendly rivals, Jack Nicklaus. The two golfing greats play against each other all the time on the Senior Tour.

Lee has always enjoyed being in the spotlight. He is outgoing and has made friends all over the world.

Lee also believes in helping others. Back in 1968, when he didn't have a lot of money, Lee won the Hawaiian Open. He gave $10,000 of his winnings to the family of Ted Makalena. Makalena was a friend and fellow golfer who died in a surfing accident.

Lee has always supported charities that benefit people of all races, religions, and ethnic backgrounds. He has devoted time and energy in support of cancer research, children's hospitals, disabled veterans, and orphanages. Lee has also invited poor children to watch him play.

Lee talks with a young fan at the 1977 British Open.

No story on Lee would be complete without mention of his longtime caddie Herman Mitchell. Herman, who weighed over 300 pounds before going on a diet, is a familiar sight to golf fans. He and Lee have a special relationship. It goes beyond boss and employee. Lee pays Herman a salary and gives him a percentage of his winnings. Not many players share their winnings with their caddies.

Lee will always be remembered for his climb to the top. He fought hard to get there and has fought hard to stay there. Lee had a brush with death when he was struck by lightning. He beat the odds that day. And he has beaten them numerous times before and since. His childhood of poverty, the back

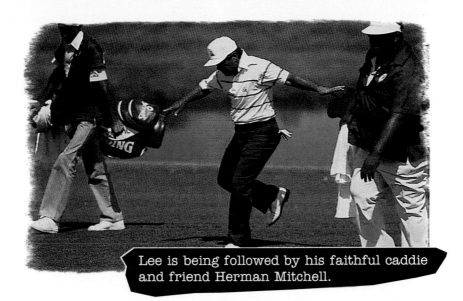

Lee is being followed by his faithful caddie and friend Herman Mitchell.

problems, the bad thumb, the neck surgery . . . it's amazing what he's endured!

"When it comes to the game of life," Lee says, "I figure I've played the whole course." He has had some ups and downs. But Lee has always come through it with a smile on his face.

"You only live once," he says. "Why not have some fun?"

Lee Trevino's Career Highlights

1960 Turns pro.

1967 Joins the PGA Tour. Finishes fifth at U.S. Open in New Jersey.

1968 Wins U.S. Open in Rochester, New York.

1970 Leads PGA Tour in earnings. Wins first of five Vardon Trophies for lowest scoring average.

1971 Wins U.S. Open, Canadian Open, and first of two British Opens.

1974 Wins PGA Championship.

1981 Elected to PGA and World Golf halls of fame.

1984 Wins second PGA Championship.

1990 Becomes first player on Senior Tour to win $1 million in a single season. Wins seven tournaments, including U.S. Senior Open.

1994 Cracks million-dollar mark for third time as a senior.

Lee Trevino's Vital Statistics

Full name: Lee Buck Trevino

Height: 5´7˝ **Weight:** 180 lb.

Birth date: December 1, 1939

Birthplace: Dallas, Texas

Residence: Jupiter Island, Florida

Family: Wife, Claudia. Six children: Richard (11/21/62), Leslie Ann (8/30/65), Tony Lee (4/13/69), Troy (9/13/73), Olivia Leigh (2/3/89), and Lee Daniel (10/20/92).

Other interests: Fishing

Joined PGA Tour: 1967

Joined Senior PGA Tour: 1989

Lee Trevino's Career Victories

PGA Tour (total of 27 wins):

1968 U.S. Open, Hawaiian Open

1969 Tucson Open

1970 Tucson Open, National Airlines Open

1971 Tallahassee Open, Danny Thomas–Memphis Classic, U.S. Open, Canadian Open, Sahara Invitational

1972 Danny Thomas–Memphis Classic, Greater Hartford Open, Greater St. Louis Classic

1973 Jackie Gleason Inverrary, Doral Eastern Open

1974 New Orleans Open, PGA Championship

1975 Florida Citrus Open

1976 Colonial National Invitational

1977 Canadian Open

1978 Colonial National Invitational

1979 Canadian Open

1980 Tournament Players Championship, Danny Thomas–Memphis Classic, San Antonio–Texas Open

1981 Tournament of Champions

1984 PGA Championship

Note: The British Open is a major event, but it isn't part of the PGA Tour.

Senior PGA Tour (total of 24 wins):

1990 Royal Caribbean Classic, Aetna Challenge, Vintage Chrysler Invitational, Doug Sanders Kingswood Celebrity Classic, NYNEX Commemorative, U.S. Senior Open, Transamerica Senior Golf Championship

1991 Aetna Challenge, Vantage at the Dominion, Sunwest Bank/Charley Pride Senior Classic

1992 Vantage at the Dominion, The Tradition, PGA Seniors Championship, Las Vegas Senior Classic, Bell Atlantic Classic

1993 Cadillac NFL Classic, Nationwide Championship, Vantage Championship

1994 Royal Caribbean Classic, PGA Seniors Championship, PaineWebber Invitational, Bell Atlantic Classic, BellSouth Senior Classic, Northville Long Island Classic

Further Reading

Blackstone, Margaret. *This Is Mini Golf.* New York: Henry Holt, 1995.

Creighton, Susan. *Greg Norman.* Mankato, MN: Crestwood House, 1988.

Gilbert, Thomas W. *Lee Trevino.* New York: Chelsea House, 1992.

Hayes, Larry, *The Junior Golf Book.* New York: St. Martin's Press, 1994.

Sanford, William R. and Carl R. Green. *Babe Didrickson Zaharias.* New York: Crestwood House, 1993.

Index

Index *cont.*